UNSPOKEN THOUGHTS

SYMPOL

Unspoken Thoughts
All Rights Reserved.
Copyright © 2017 Sympol
v3.0

The opinions expressed in this manuscript are solely the opinions of the author and do not represent the opinions or thoughts of the publisher. The author has represented and warranted full ownership and/or legal right to publish all the materials in this book.

This book may not be reproduced, transmitted, or stored in whole or in part by any means, including graphic, electronic, or mechanical without the express written consent of the publisher except in the case of brief quotations embodied in critical articles and reviews.

U-BLU-IT Publishing

ISBN: 978-0-578-18883-6

Cover Photo © 2017 thinkstockphotos.com. All rights reserved - used with permission.

PRINTED IN THE UNITED STATES OF AMERICA

I want to thank everyone who put their ingredients into this pot of gumbo, also known as my life: my mother (Chop), both sides of my family (the Blus & DeHons), much love forever; R.I.P. my grandmother (mama), my grandfather (Paw Paw), my cousins (Tina, Brandye, Sandra); major love to the hood that put the most spice in this gumbo . . . the East Side of Indianapolis, 46th and Arlington, all I have to say is bars and vogues, East Side Skating Rink, and 38th Street Car Wash for Life . . . Thanks for the help raising me.

IN MEMORY

Mama

IN MEMORY

Paw Paw

IN MEMORY

Tina

TABLE OF CONTENTS

PROTECTION	1
THEY CALL ME SYMPOL	2
SECRET	3
RUSSIAN ROULETTE	4
HOOKS IN YOU	5
SAY, MAN	6
BABIES HAVING BABIES	7
KNOCK, KNOCK	8
IN MEMORY	9
HE LOVES HER (JESUS)	10
GOING DOWN	11
JUSTIFY	12
I WATCH	13
HATER	14
QUIVERS, SHAKES AND SHIVERS	15
WHAT DO YOU SEE?	16
AM I	17
LOST BOY	18
PLAYER OR NOT?	19
HE HATES	20
TRAMP	22
HOLIDAY	23
SELLOUT	24
HOOD RAT	25
GIVING IN	26
PLAYING HOOKY	27
WHIGGA (WHITE NIGGA)	28
WHAT TEAM	29
CHRISTMAS LIST	30
CHOICES	32

PETAL	33
ANDRE HARRIS	34
FAMILY TREE	35
HOW IT STARTS	36
TO MY BLACK WOMEN	37
GAMES	39
A GLIMPSE	40
TRASH OR TREASURE	41
LOSER ME	42
WELCOME!!!	43
WORTH IT?	44
"I WANT"	46
CANNABIS	47
FETISH	48
SO FINE	49
FRIENDS (KIDS)	50
COMPANY	51
HOME SWEET HOME?	52
MASQUERADE	53
DO THE MATH (2+2=?)	54
FRIEND OR WIFE/FUTURE OR PAST	55
TEAR	56
NO!	57
RUTHLESS	58
WHAT COUNTS?	59
ANY GIVEN SUNDAY	60
OPPOSITES DON'T ATTRACT?	61
WHAT'S HER NAME?	62
AFFAIR TO REMEMBER	63
VICARIOUS	64
YES	65
UP CLOSE & PERSONAL	66

CONFESSIONS	67
JUNKYARD	68
NOTHING LASTS	69
RUNAWAY	70
HIMSELF	71
ANGEL	72
'80S KINGS	73
TRENDS	74
WISH (OR DO I?)	75
HANGMAN	76
"WOW"	77
CAN'T STOP	78
YOU TELL ME!	79
LOOKING AHEAD	80
ARE YOU AFRAID?	81
REGRETS	82
ROSALINDA	83
RARE FIND	84
ALONE	85
COWARD?	86
SILENT NIGHT	87
"NO TRUST, NO PEACE"	88
DEAR GOD	89
END TIMES	90
WITHDRAW	91
FRIEND OR FOE–(HO)	92
WASTED YOUTH	94
IN STYLE	95
ONE LAST BREATH	96
SIGHT UNSEEN	97
WE SHINE IN THE DARK	98
SEASONS	99

REFLECTIONS	100
CANDY	101
YOUNG BOYS	103
YOUNG BOYS, STOP IMITATING A THUG	104
HALF-MAST	105
BLESSED	106

PROTECTION

When you read this book from start to finish
And from finish to start
You will understand
Why I wear a condom on my heart

THEY CALL ME SYMPOL

They call me Sympol . . . It's a metaphor because my Poetry
Is simple but with a few twists and turns.
I'm a complicated man . . . Such as a Rubik's cube
Is a simple square but with a few twists and turns . . .
It's complicated to understand.
Just as pyramids are a simple triangle and yet it
Baffles man to this day.
Such as, it's simple to understand prayer, but you can't
Fathom how God hears one out of millions when you pray.
Like it's simple to understand that a cow goes moo,
A pig goes oink, and a duck goes quack
But it is difficult to understand why a white swan is born to this
earth black
I just want to unite all people . . . it's that <u>simple</u>, that's all.
I just want to bring all people together like the fall of the Berlin Wall.
There are those of you out there who will get this and you are on
the right path.
And then there are those of you out there who are clueless
Like a gorilla in the Congo scratching his ass.
So to put it simply, I'm Symply the best!
The person who loves to hear me speak the most . . .
I found out she's DEAF!
Is that too complicated or is that too simple?
Don't feel **simple**-minded if that riddle makes you scratch your
temple!
<u>That's</u> why they call me Sympol!

SECRET

I've got a secret eating my Liver inside.
You stare at me, yet you can't see it in my eyes.
You would Love to know what this is all about?
Here's a hint, you can smell the secret coming out of my mouth!
Millions have the same secret as me.
As "AA," I know they would agree.
I can't live with this secret, yet I can't live without it.
Will I ever let this secret out? I doubt it!
Don't you have a clue when I slur my words?
Don't you have a clue when I stumble down the curb?
Don't you have a clue when I call in to work sick?
Don't you have a clue when I scream, "I'm not Drunk, Bitch!"?
Hey, World, I've got a Secret,
And I just might die trying to keep it!!
SHHHHHHH!

RUSSIAN ROULETTE

I can't put that thing on because I can't feel the sex.
After it's all said and done, you lie on your back having regrets.
Why is it after the second encounter we won't wear that thing
like we know we should?
Just hoping she didn't get AIDS while sleeping with the boys in
the hood.
Why do we get so complacent after the sex encounters total three?
As if, you didn't get sick after the first two times
so he or she must be HIV-free.
After Kelly, Lisa, Kim, and Amy, you still lie on your back with regrets.
After Tasha, Rita, Shannon, you still play Russian roulette.
I know this is a song that over and over and over you've heard sang.
But eventually you will hear click, click, click,
BANG!

HOOKS IN YOU

While your wife is at church Sunday praying for you to stop sinning
You're at a massage parlor trying to get a happy ending.
Hooks In You
Ten minutes into your daughter's recital
You think that bottle of gin in your car is oh so vital.
Hooks In You
Her husband works two jobs and tried to make every penny count
But she secretly embezzles his money into her personal bank account
Hooks In You
He can have his hooks in me, his hooks in him, his hooks in her
Just know that no one is immune to the hooks of Lucifer.

SAY, MAN

Say, man, and I use that term loosely,
Ever since we were 16 years old you've been cool with me.
But out of us Thugs, you were the one everybody considered so nice,
The soft-hearted one, the intellectual.
Now some years later, you want to come out of the closet
and tell me you're a homosexual?
Say man, and again I use the term loosely,
If that's what you've chosen it doesn't matter that I disagree.
I guess you lied about all the women in the stories you would tell.
I'd have to say, you did hide it well!
Emotionally, I can't imagine what you were going through.
The question is, were you born like this or did you choose?
An insecure man would walk away for good and wish
you would get what you deserve.
But you were cool then, and you're cool now,
so I ain't going to kick you to the curb.
But because I say, "It's your life if that's how you want to live it."
Don't call telling me your business thinking that I'm cool with it.
Just keep your head up, and I don't mean that figuratively.
I mean it literally.

BABIES HAVING BABIES

You're just a child,
How can you raise a child?
It's a shame you're doing your homework
While that child screams out loud.
Your mom, she can't lend you a helping hand,
She's at her second job trying to support you,
Your child, and her alcoholic man.
Still in your early teens, what the hell are you
Going to do?
Take the baby to school for show and tell?
You thought it was cool,
You just couldn't wait to show it.
Now you're angry, lost, scared
But not wanting your friends to know it.
School dance—I think not
Pep rally—I think not.
Fifteen years old and you already know what it
Feels like to be distraught.
Your mother never finished school,
Now neither will you.
The cycle repeats itself,
Your child is already set up to lose.
That's not a legacy to be handed down
From generation to generation.
Stop the madness!!!

KNOCK, KNOCK

Damn! I thought that the battle was over.
It's been three and a half years sober.
But now it's come creeping back into my life,
Stoppin' by to visit for the past month every night.
Temptation, Temptation, Temptation.
Its knocks become louder and louder.
Three and a half years sober—I couldn't be prouder.
Now I'm unsure what the future has in store.
As temptation knocks it becomes harder to ignore.
How much longer until I open the front door?
Even if tonight's temptation walks away, at some
Point she will return again,
Knocking on the door as I look through the peephole
And see the bottle of gin.
A situation that seems almost impossible to win.
Knock!
…….Knock!
………..Knock!

IN MEMORY

Whether this is wrong or whether this is right,
I can't believe you snuck out of the house tonight.
Simply put . . . damn, you're bold.
Sneaking out like a teenager, even though you're thirty years old.
Tell me, does it turn you on the way we keep creeping?
Or is it that your husband is a few feet away in the house sleeping?
You cover my mouth with your breast and whisper, "No more questions."
Little did I know that tonight we would both learn a valuable lesson.
I taste your sweat, you swallow my soul.
Up and down faster and faster we go.
The windows steamed up.
The car rocking side to side.
Oh shit! It's your husband peeking
Inside my ride!
BANG!
Darkness,
Go to the light.
Go to the light.
Go to the light.

HE LOVES HER (JESUS)

No more public transportation
Now she has money to buy her son the shoes he needs
The coat plus a new PlayStation
HE LOVES HER (Jesus)
No more working 3 jobs breaking her neck
No more continuously asking the loser to please
Send a child support check
HE LOVES HER (Jesus)
No more borrowing a cup of sugar or a glass of milk
Or even 3 dollars from the lady next door
He loves her, He loves me, and He loves you
Once she gave her problems to GOD
Those are problems that she no longer goes through
She knows life still has its ups and downs
Now when she encounters turbulence
All she can do is smile
HE LOVES HER (Jesus)

GOING DOWN

I bob up, I sink under
I bob up, I sink under
I know that they see me, why won't they help I wonder
I almost dislocate my shoulder trying 2 extend my hand
No one wants 2 take hold I don't understand
I go down, I come up, I see friends
I go down, I come up, I see family
Are they willing 2 stand by and watch this travesty
Is this the thanks I get from all of y'all
2 stand by and watch me drown in this sea of alcohol
Each time I resurface 4 air
I get a glimpse of people that don't seem 2 care
Once again I see family and friends
The current is sweeping me under, is this the end?
Seconds before I black out,
I swear on some of their faces I see a grin

JUSTIFY

How can you justify judging me and judging she
When you put her into the life of luxury
and me in the life of poverty?
And yet you judge by the same set of rules,
I have to say I do think that is cruel.
Justify.
It's said that I have freedom to choose,
but if it's the wrong path I choose, guess what?
I Lose.
No matter what my child did,
I could never throw him into a pit of fire.
And yet I'm only human and you're God
so how can you do that to me, if you desire?
Justify.
Poverty, alcohol, rape, murder, drugs;
Growing up with no hugs
And I'm expected to walk a straight line
in a crooked world that shows me no love?
Justify.
If Jesus were here today, could he once again walk this world
on the path you say is right?
I'll save that question
for when I'm down on my knees tomorrow night.

I WATCH

I sit outside the hospital
On the day you were born and my soul is torn
(I watch)

Years later I sit outside
Observing your first day of school
Feeling the part of a fool
(I watch)

I observe you make your first
Touchdown in junior high
But me, I'm still living a lie
(I watch)

I see you walk across the graduation stage
Yet I still can't turn the page
(I watch)

You stand in your tuxedo
About to marry your beautiful bride
As I look from the back of the church
Heart filled with pride
(I watch)

Though I know it's not logical
Do I tell you I'm your biological?

HATER

I used to be 18, 20, 23, and 25 years old.
Would dare anybody to bring it to me in the streets
because I was just that cold; just that bold.
Now I see you do the same, and I say,
"Dumb nigga" . . . Am I a hater?
I used to have the gold, the body muscles
walking around with no shirt.
Calling women bitches; treating them like dirt.
Now I see you do the same,
I say, "Dumb nigga" . . . Am I a hater?
I used to have the gangsta car with the rims, the paint,
and the music bumping out loud.
Turning heads as I pass by a crowd.
Now I see you do the same
and I say, "Dumb nigga" . . . Am I a hater?

QUIVERS, SHAKES AND SHIVERS

Waking up early in the morning with the shakes from the liquor
They said I'd be a loser; their wishes came true I figure
QUICK!! I take a sip to gain my composure
My hands shake as I put them together
to pray one day I hope to have closure
An end to this liquid that measures a pint
An end to this juice that won't allow me to participate in life
Unable to take out the trash I'm overcome by anxiety
So in this room I sit alone, at peace as long as this bottle is beside me
My best friend yet at the same time my worst enemy
At times it's the source of my peace
At times it's the source of my hostility
As my sips increase, my shakes start to leave
Is it even worth another night asking for help down on my knees?

WHAT DO YOU SEE?

Money, I don't have it.
Homes, Cars, and Assets are something that I can always acquire.
But Men with all that, to get what I have, would sell their
Soul to the Devil and be willing to perish in the Fire.
I'm Rich beyond belief.
But with something you Gold Diggers can't see.
I have a Loving Heart, I'm Committed, Faithful, plus Loyal.
And my Love for the Lord Burns so Hot I can bring
ice water to a Boil.
I used to be a Thug.
Now the only Gang Signs I'm throwing up is the Peace Sign,
Because I'm only Banging Love.
I use to be a Drunk.
But now I'm protected with every step I take because
My Guardian Angel hovers above
My face which is like a shell, it's just an outer.
And honestly, sometimes I'm intimidated to approach you
because I know I'm not Fine, and I don't think you could
Laugh any Louder.
If I could only take a Magic Wand and turn my Body inside
out, to where you couldn't see the outer but only the inner.
I guarantee you'd see a 6-Figure Winner.

AM I

Am I wrong to want everybody to feel the pain I've felt?
Am I wrong to want everybody to play the hand that I was dealt?
Am I wrong to want everybody to put a smile on their face
Even though it feels like you've just been pepper sprayed with Mace?
Am I wrong to want everybody to know the feeling
Of having your dreams severely crushed
And know the dependency of using dope
or the bottle as such a crutch?
Am I wrong?
Am I?
Am I?
Answer Me!!!!!

LOST BOY

10 years old
A new football only nobody to catch it
Lost boy

11 years old
A new baseball bat and glove, only nobody to hit the ball
Lost boy

12 years old
A new soccer ball, only no one to kick it to
Lost boy

13 years old
A new basketball, only no one to block the shot
Lost boy

14 years old
New pent-up anger, only this time
There's a street gang to show him how to use it
BE A FATHER!!!!!!!!!!!

PLAYER OR NOT?

I was a player who jumped from club to club
Women to women
And bed to bed
Until I found gray hairs on top
And the sides of my head
But I'm a player
And this game I won't take a loss
So I decided 2 simply shave them off
The very next year
What did appear?
Yes, more gray hairs
In my beard
Again, I'm a player
And this game I won't take a loss
And again, I decided 2 shave them off
Again the next year
Fumbling to put on my underwear
Oh yes, I discovered
Gray hair down there
But I'm a player
And this game I won't take a loss
So I decided the player's lifestyle
Is not worth this cost

Know when to quit!

HE HATES

He hates to wake up
To his alarm clock screaming B-U-Z-Z
But as soon as it does
He starts searching for a buzz
You see, he hates his life
Be it wrong or be it right
He's tired of hearing himself whining
He's tired of the grey clouds in his life
And always trying to find the silver lining

He's tired of hearing from his family,
His friends, and all the rest
That this is another one of God's tests

You see, he hates his life
Years ago he decided to change and move out of the hood
But all of his thug friends
Are eating lobster, and he's still eating canned goods
He's tried the right way for oh so long
Yet at the end of the day,
He keeps hearing the same sad song

You see, he hates his life
He's tired of hearing that God won't give you more
Than you can bear
Now look deep into his eyes,
He no longer cares
Now he just sits on the couch
With a bottle of gin up to his mouth

You see, he hates his life
He looks at his gun, his ski mask, and his knife
Whichever one he chooses
I wouldn't blame him because,
You see, I too hate my life

TRAMP

What went wrong in her life
To make her want to destroy an
Unborn child's life?
Tramp!

How could she put that
Cigarette up to her lips?

She might as well put it
In between her legs
That some call a clit.
Tramp!

The audacity of her
To inhale that smoke
How could she take her unborn
Child's life as a joke?
Tramp!

As a parent, I know she would be negligent

Why, you ask?
Because she's smoking while
She's pregnant.
Tramp!

So, 911 I dialed
Because she was
Endangering the life of a child
Tramp!

HOLIDAY

Oh, how she loves the holidays
But she's a widow and all alone.

So she calls 911
Just to have someone
to talk to on the phone

That's the sad reality of
The life she's living

Have a Happy Thanksgiving!

SELLOUT

So let me get this straight
I'm a sellout, and it's me that you hate
Because I left the hood
Where all through my childhood I was no damn good
Sellout because now I can see the mountains and see the leaves change
As of before I could see the graffiti, smell the piss, and on the corner 24/7 I would hang
Sellout because on Friday night with my wife at an Italian restaurant
With a bottle of wine
Instead of being on the corner with you and a bottle of wine
Sellout because I want to sit at home in front of the fireplace
Or because I don't sit and smoke fire at your place
Sellout because I want to go to the club and listen to jazz
Or because I don't want to go to your club where the last time I got
Stabbed—you do the math
What you don't understand is the whole part of thug life
Is to get the money so you can get out of the hood.
Am I wrong or Am I right?
But to me, the part that is really absurd
Is you want to live in the hood
Only you grew up in an Indiana suburb

HOOD RAT

Why are you 38 years old and still have a ringtone on your phone?
Why in 1 year's time you have had three different men living in your home?
HOOD RAT, HOOD RAT
So busy worrying about how you're going to get paid
So that you can pay for your man's fade and even your braids
That you overlooked your child's failing grades
HOOD RAT, HOOD RAT
You took your boyfriend's side when your daughter told you she was abused
Now she dresses like a dude because she is confused
HOOD RAT, HOOD RAT
You told your son that he was a pussy when he showed any fears
Now he's a bigger pussy in prison for the next 40 years
HOOD RAT, HOOD RAT
But you did attempt to go to the church seeking help from the pastor
But, oops, she had sex with him and now she is pregnant with her 3rd little bastard
HOOD RAT, HOOD RAT

GIVING IN

Black woman, black woman, black woman, you have come too far
Just to settle for that man that puts his whole paycheck into his car.
I know times have changed and now you have a college degree
So please stop settling for somebody like me.
Now you have your own house and credit, a large amount,
And he, me, or we don't even have a bank account.
Do a background check . . . See how far back he is on his child support.
He has no problem remembering your payday
Yet can't remember what day he's due in court.
Even though your future is bright and his future is dim,
He has no problem approaching you because he knows the pickings are slim.
Locked up, dope dealing, or gay . . . it's not all true.
Black woman, black woman, take your time and keep your cool.
Don't just settle on any old fool.
I have a sister, cousins, and women friends that are just plain cool,
So if you think I'm player hatin', you must be one of those losers I'm talking to.

PLAYING HOOKY

She meets me outside of the school gym door
She looks so good the next stop is the liquor store.
A little intoxication can't do us much harm
I sent the neighborhood drunk to buy us a bottle of Boones Farm.
Walking deep into the woods, hand in hand
I love looking into her hazel eyes, my friends wouldn't understand.
I love the residue from her lip gloss on the top of the wine bottle
I love taking off her letterman sweater
Because she looks like a lingerie model.
On my neck and hers scorched is a big red hickey
O-my God, girl, I love playing hooky.
After it's all said and done
I'll see you at the homecoming game tonight
And yes, we will be dressed alike

Pinky Swear
1986

WHIGGA (WHITE NIGGA)

Whigga, whigga, white nigga.
Riding around listening to Nas, Tupac, or Jigga.
You thought acting black was cool.
I guess it started back in jr. high school.
I have no problem with skin color
Do your thing if it's wanting to be like another
You claim you're in a gang, listen to rap music, and wear baggy clothes
You say nigga, throw up gang signs, and call girls bitches and hoes
You make fun of your white counterparts
Roll your eyes and neck and talk like you got heart
You wear your hair in braids or even a fade
That person of color over there last night you claim you laid
But it's all good in the hood
Or at least it should
But 10 years have passed, and you have changed
Now you want to be called by your birth name
Now you have a college degree
Now you don't know your homies in the hood that look like me
That picture you loved of you and black homeboys don't sit on your desk
It's your Alpha Cum Laude frat brothers in the same frame the picture rests.

WHAT TEAM

This is a situation that I just can't ignore
Me and many others want to know what team do you play for
You see on the streets and in the club you portray yourself to be so hard
Yet my eyes and ears in prison say that you were having sex with other men behind bars
So what team do you play for?
Walkin' around out here like an alpha male
Now it's starting to make sense why in jail you never wanted anybody to pay your bail
So what team do you play for?
Even if I had life in prison with no chance of parole
Down that road I could not go
So what team do you play for?
You see
That's how HIV runs rampant through our community
I've heard this rumor more than twice
And you been in prison more than twice
The reason I'm concerned is because my sister is your wife
So what team do you play for?

CHRISTMAS LIST

My Christmas list, my Christmas wish
Is that I get back the six years
Of my son's life that I missed

Question, "What did I do to deserve this?"

Second is to accept that the first
Will never be granted

Now I am in his life
Let me help him grow
Because his seed, I did help plant it

Though my impressions and values
Were not instilled upon him at birth
Let me vanquish and deprogram
Any negativity and filth he's absorbed
From the earth

Let him accept the fact it's my blood
That runs through his veins
Although when he speaks of his father
He speaks another man's name

I know it was a sin to engage with this woman
Who in God's eyes is married
But is this burden payback?
Is this the burden that I will carry?

This Christmas, let it rain
In place of snow

So when I cry outside
No one will know

Merry Christmas to all
And to all a good night

Santa, can you please bring some joy to me
On this silent night?

CHOICES

I've got a strange insight that my life is about to expire
So I only felt it right that at this time I express my desire.
I have loved you from day one.
Oh, how I wished that you were the mother of my son.
You would talk to me for an hour about your man's misbehaving ways.
I would talk to God for an hour about you as I pray.
This connection between us, me and you, you and I.
I know he has to see it when he watches us look into each other's eyes.
Do you think of me when you're lying next to him?
I think of you when I'm lying next to what's her name . . .
Oh yeah, Kim.
I have a junior high school crush only I'm a grown man.
I want to tell my homeboy about you only you are his woman and he wouldn't understand.
I know Karma is coming back to bite me, but I have to take that chance.
Man, oh man, the games people play when it comes to romance.
My heart bleeds for him, yet my soul yearns for you.
In this dangerous game of choices, Baby,
I choose you.

PETAL

Today I found a single rose petal
Under what used to be our bed
It's dry
It's dusty
And it's been long dead
The only remaining evidence
Of our last night together
Rings were exchanged
And promises were made
To become one forever
But whoever expected my doorbell to ring
On the other side of that door was a woman named Christine
A woman from my past
A woman with no class
She had a beautiful body
And a whole lot of charm
But you wanted to know why
She was holding an infant child in her arms
So I tried to explain
But written all over your face
Was nothing but pain
Her last words to me were
She could not believe it
After I confessed that yes,
I had cheated
It turns out the child does not share my DNA
It's been one year and
I still search for you every day
All I have are the memories that linger
But they're starting to crumple like this dead rose petal
Between my fingers

ANDRE HARRIS

The last time that I cried was 1987
When my best friend died
He took his last breath
While I was holding his hand
And people wonder
Why I question God's plan

It was supposed to be me
In the backseat of the car that night
So now I wonder why
Why did God spare my life?

R.I.P Dre

That summer of 1987 was cut short
Because God took away the
Life from your heart

You picking me up
On your moped from my first job
Who would ever have thought
That summer your life would be robbed?

I know we were the cool crowd
But this pain
I can no longer mask it
Because it's a week before school starts
And I'm carrying your casket

FAMILY TREE

My family tree was planted on top of a landfill
What grew was alcoholism, tar-filled lungs, and anti-depressant pills
From a distance, it stands tall, healthy, and beautiful
But up close, it's withered, termite-infested, and the wood is no longer useful
Not even birds would dare build a nest
When the leaves fall, you can't tell the difference from the trash on the ground that was once left
Is it the stench from the leaves or the stench from the trash that is buried beneath?
No animals hang around from a squirrel to a leech
Even trash men won't sit under it and eat their lunch
So groundsmen cut it down because me, my family, and this tree have suffered way 2 much

HOW IT STARTS

It started with a hug
That turned into love.
Then that same love turned into a mean mug.
Then that turned into a shove.
That's how it starts!
Next comes the torn shirt.
Then your first excuse that he just had a bad day at work.
That's how it starts!
Then comes the tears.
Next comes the second excuse that he had too many beers.
That's how it starts!
Next comes your first fight.
Then comes the sunglasses at night.
That's how it starts!
Then comes explaining the bloodstains on your pants.
Next comes the ride in the ambulance.
That's how it starts!
Then comes your family putting flowers in the dirt
After you just took a ride in the hearse.
That's how it ends!

TO MY BLACK WOMEN

To my black women out there
Holding down your household
You are in charge.

Beware . . . There's a lot of gold diggin'
Brothers out here at large.
I know you need lovin'
And time away from the kids alone.
I know you need to hear a tender voice
Asking, How was your day?
Over the phone.

Some ignorant ass just might laugh.
But I know you would love a man to run you a bath.
The child's father has up and ran,
Which could leave you extremely bitter
Toward a man.

Yet and still I give you all the credit
For not selling out.
Waiting for love and still knowing
What family is all about.

Not giving up your bed to the first man
That comes along with a smile on his face
And a real sad song.

Knowing that it is your child
That truly comes first.
Able to spot any con man's line in a club
That's definitely been rehearsed.

How can you raise a man?
You weren't born a man.
But giving 150% doing the best
That you can.

God brings help to those truly in need,
Hold on, be strong—
Help is on its way.
Trust in me.

GAMES

Why? Why? Why won't you let me in? Is it me or the power
I once had over you?
Is it all the crazy love games I took you through?
Or all the feelings that I made you prove?
Don't let your feelings be clouded by anger.
Let me in, it's not as if you are in some kind of danger.
Like when you were pregnant and I offered you a hanger.
The halo hovering above your head no longer appears.
The fire that burned in your eyes has now been
Extinguished by tears.
Is this the legacy that I will leave for you?
A trail of broken promises from an immature fool
Careless handling of your feelings contributed into you
Morphing into this block of ice.
Because of me playing with your heart
as if it were a game of dice.
Now I realize my love for you leaves little to no doubt.
But it's a little too late and I guess the game is over because I
Just crapped out.

A GLIMPSE

Never ever ever did I understand cheating on your wife
Until I got a quick inside view of the married life
I had to live under her roof for just one month
And truthfully that was three weeks too much
I try to have a conversation on the phone with my best friend
And I see her reflection in the mirror doing her best to listen in
I can't sit down to read the paper or watch TV
Without her peeking over her shoulder at me
I stay up too late, I cut the grass wrong, I bought the wrong brand of trash bag
PICK PICK PICK NAG NAG NAG
Now by no means are these reasons to cheat on your wife
With that being said, all of this stress after only four weeks in my life
My view on marriage has been permanently scarred
A love that's meant for you should not be this hard
I'm not using these as excuses, I'm not that kind of man
But to some of my cheating brothers out there
let's just say I do understand

TRASH OR TREASURE

The night before Christmas Eve
And I'm at home all alone
My friend calls to say he's
With a woman from the club about to cheat on his wife
Oh what I wouldn't give to have his married life
A great family at home
And he's out trying to get some extra pleasure
I guess it's true
One man's Trash is another man's Treasure

LOSER ME

WE JUST HAD SEX,
WITH A SMILE ON YOUR FACE,
YOUR HAND IN MY HAND, YOU ROLL OVER,
WITH A FROWN ON MY FACE,
MY HAND LEAVES YOUR HAND, AND I SAY,
IT'S OVER!
I REALIZED LOOKING AT YOU I SEE HER FACE
WHEN KISSING YOU IT IS HER I TASTE.
I KNOW IT'S A TRAVESTY, I KNOW IT'S A SHAME,
I KNEW IT WAS OVER WHEN I DID ALL IN MY POWER
NOT TO SCREAM HER NAME.
IT WAS NOT MY INTENT
TO END IT LIKE THIS.
MY INTENT WAS TO SIMPLY
END THIS WITH A KISS.
NOW LYING IN THIS BED WITH HER, JAZZ, WINE,
AND FEELING MELLOW
UNEASY BECAUSE I STILL SMELL YOUR TEARDROPS
ON MY PILLOW.

WELCOME!!!

January 22, 2001
Born into this world
He is here at last
My beautiful son.

As you exit the womb
I anticipate my face to be
The first that you see in
The hospital room.

Regrettably, let me
Be the first
To welcome you
To HELL!

I only wish you
Could understand me
Because I have 8 million
Stories to tell.

January 23, 2001,
From here forth you're
Suppose to grow such as a flower
And bloom.

But the stories
I have to tell
Will make you
Want to reenter that womb.
Welcome to Hell!
I love you.

WORTH IT?

From time to time you would say,
"I only sneak just a little bit,"
But here's a checklist for you to find out,
Was the sneaking truly worth it?

Court-issued appointments
For you and your child to play
Only to come back from the park
To find Mr. Mr.'s car in your ex-wife's driveway.
(Was it worth it?)

Now Mr. Mr. is helping your child
Fly their first kite.
So tell me, was it worth all the creeping
And sneaking late nights?

Now you know the feeling of dropping
Your child off on a Sunday afternoon
Overcome by grief because it's just too soon.
(Was it worth it?)

So tell me, were these other women worth all this;
The fireplace, the tree, and the presents
And Mr. Mr. with your child on Christmas?
(Was it worth it?)

Reminiscing on all the women you used to devour
Now on Christmas Day alone
Drinking an egg nog that's sour.
(Was it worth it?)

Starting to recall all the hopes you had
On your wedding night
As your child opens their present
From Mr. Mr., and guess what?
It's their first bike.
(Was it worth it?)

"I WANT"

I'm ready to do it right.
I want to wake up with my Family and go to bed
With my Family every Night.
I want to do yard work on the Weekends.
I want to eat Sunday Dinner with you and the kids.
I want to sit on the Toilet and talk about our day
While you simultaneously take a bath.
I want to help with Dinner while you help our child
with his Math.
I want you to ask me if your dress matches your purse
As you straighten my tie while we are getting ready for Church.
Damn, I screwed up my Future
with the past life I was livin'.
Damn, I hate I have two kids by two different women.
Do I still have a chance at that Dream?
Or is it Just another Fantasy?
So, Lord, this is my wish list that I'll be sending.
But so far, so much for my Happy Ending!

CANNABIS

When I was introduced to you, I was not so sure
I heard that you were fun, but I didn't know
if it was something that I could endure
I gave you a chance
Before I knew it,
this had blossomed into a hell of a romance
You made everything so funny
I was your man, and you were my honey
In you I invested a lot of time and a lot of money
You made the world a different place
When I was with you,
our feelings were written all over our face
You made my world go BANG!
Before you came along, how in the world did I hang?
But suddenly, you changed
When we were around other people,
you just made me want to laugh
Now around people
You just make me want to dash
You make me second guess myself
When I used to be confident
You used to make me feel like a king
Now you make me feel like I ain't shit
Why did you change?
With you I can no longer hang
I keep coming back hoping things will be like old times,
But now you just constantly manipulate my mind
All you do is bring me paranoia
I'm going to do my best to destroy 'ya
So I open the bag and throw you down the toilet
There, I destroyed it

FETISH

A drug addict's vein fiends for the heroin.
A smoker's lungs scream for the nicotine.
An alcoholic's liver cries for the juice.
Nymphomaniacs lust for the sexual fruits.

A black man's impure thoughts
Toward a white woman named Heather,
Ask yourself, what's your pleasure?
Fetish!

SO FINE

First off, I am in no way hesitant to speak my mind and say,
"Damn, God has made a wonderful specimen."
From the top of your naturally curly hair
To the bronze of your skin tone.
It's no wonder all of the opposite sex find it hard to leave you alone.
So smooth and calculating, and everything you do is so precise.
Let them beg, let them beg, but in your own time
Because you choose wisely.
How many times have you walked by a crowd and heard the
Whispers, "Damn, I wish you were mine."
Five words: eye candy for the blind.
Oh, what a reward to wake up and see you every morning.
To the undeserving, it must be alarming to wonder "what did
you do to deserve this?"
Then, with the preciseness of my ear, I hear a voice calling,
"Chris, Chris."
I must respond to the voice I hear.
Gently, I put down the brush and walk away from the mirror.

FRIENDS (KIDS)

I wanna hold her hand and walk by the lake
But my friends said she's fake.
I wanna open her car door
But my friends said why, she's just a whore.
I wanna make her my wife
But my friends said that I'm going to screw up my life.
Now it's our 20th anniversary and me and her both shed a tear
But none of my friends are here.
Don't continuously keep so-called friends like that around
Keep so-called friends like that where they belong,
And that's the playground.

COMPANY

She's so proud that she hasn't had a drink in one year
But he asked her to go to the liquor store
And buy him a bottle of beer.
It's been three years since she has had a smoke
Yet he sends her to the store to buy him some cigarettes
And laughs like it's a joke
Don't give up
Because misery loves you know what.

HOME SWEET HOME?

Graffiti infiltrates the walls.
The smell of piss up and down the halls.
Yet it feels like home.
Not carpet or linen but concrete and steel
are all that my feet and naked skin feel.
Yet it feels like home.
No singing, no privacy in the shower.
It's a place where hopes and dreams get devoured.
Yet it feels like home.
No sounds of crickets chirping at night.
Only rats and roaches starting up fights.
Yet it feels like home.
Devastation, penetration, masturbation, ejaculation.
Home Sweet Home.
Mi casa es su casa?

MASQUERADE

Why are you surprised to see a Frown when you raise up my Clown Mask?

If there was a Smile, why would I need a Mask?

"Think about it!"

DO THE MATH (2+2=?)

I squeeze the trigger
BANG!
Now I'm in prison
And my life has changed.

Or has it remained the same?

You do the math.

FRIEND OR WIFE/FUTURE OR PAST

Commitments were never made
Therefore commitments would never be broken.

Subsequently along the line,
My soul starting hoping.

Funny that my old friend
Became the new lady that had been chosen.

Though I'm not in love I am in care.

Loving to play games,
But with this woman playing a game
Would be equal to accepting a dare.

On one hand excitement,
On the other hand fear.
Could she be the finest one in a line of many,
Or would this just be another wasted year?
"If so, do I shed a tear?"

No one knows what the future holds.
I would love mine to end,
With my lips kissing the tip of her nose.
As I say goodnight to my wife.

TEAR

One large drop of water hits my windshield as I sit at a stoplight.
I know something was not right.
I look up and out my sun roof, not a cloud in the sky.
I wonder, could it have been a teardrop from God's eye?

NO!

My eyes can hear
My ears can see
My mouth can smell
My nose can taste
If this makes sense to you
Then a mind is a terrible thing to waste
Drugs
Just Say No!

RUTHLESS

Girl, you know I've been thuggin' my whole unbalanced life.
Now you want to change me because you've become my wife.
Don't you see that ain't right?
I met ya how I met ya, I will keep ya how I keep ya
And I will never try to deceive ya!
You know the old saying, "What you see is what you get!"
So quit playing with fire before I leave your ass, bitch!
These thoughts ran through my head as my wife said good night.
Will this marriage last if I'm having these thoughts on my honeymoon night?

WHAT COUNTS?

Inside or out

At this moment I love everything about your soul,
Your body and your face.

Shocking to me and others
You are not of my race.

Though this feels like something sent from God,
You are not of my faith.

What does it all mean?
Let me explain.

This is something many people have experienced
Time and time again.

My eyes are blind to the color of your skin
And the church you attend.

This is a true love that grew from two true friends.
So, from what I gather,
It's the inside that counts,
And the outside does not matter.

ANY GIVEN SUNDAY

Late this Sunday night
I wonder, oh, I wonder
As I lie in my bed and listen to the thunder.

Not long ago,
Yet it seems like an eternity.
I gave you a secret code
For you and me.
That we would always think
Of one another on
Any rainy Sunday night.

No matter if there was a husband
Or if there was a wife.

So, on this rainy Sunday
With so many memories that will linger,
I wonder, do you still remember us,
Even though you now have
A ring on your finger?

OPPOSITES DON'T ATTRACT?

I would sell my soul just to have one more night in your arms.
Even if I knew the repercussions would bring me harm.
To have you on top of my body, as your necklace dangles in my face, and sparkling in my eyes, is its charm.
To hug the curves of your body, the way a glove hugs the fingers of your hand.
Only I taste a dish and say it's spicy, you taste the same and say it's bland.
We go to the beach and all I see is the Ocean, and all You see is Sand.
I Lust for the Rain.
You Lust for the Sun.
How can I accept the end to this relationship that you claim never truly begun?

WHAT'S HER NAME?

To know your name is only to be hopeful,
Equivalent to knowing one of life's little secrets.
Like why is the wind invisible?

Will I be given a chance to give this woman
Memories that linger?
Or as I approach and get close,
Will there be a ring upon her finger?

Do I approach you or not,
Do I turn or do I stay?
I'm like a fragile tree on a windy day,

I sway, back and forth, right to left.
Could this be the start of my love's birth,
Or the start of its death?

AFFAIR TO REMEMBER

We haven't spent that much time alone,
Yet and still when you're in my arms
I feel right at home.

Though a religious man,
When it comes to you
I feel the urge to commit a sin.

I love watching this relationship grow,
And hope it will never end.

This relationship that we've portrayed,
Gets harder and harder because
Promises were never made.

This man needs more than
Just the linger of your perfume.
But unable to reach you
Because you're at home
With another man sleeping in the same room.

(You know who you are)

VICARIOUS

You live vicariously through me
I live vicariously through you
It's crazy what life puts us through
That's why everybody wants 2 B someone else
Nobody wants 2 B them self

YES

Yes! It's too much to ask
That I never speak
Of the woman in my past.

Yes! It's too much that I
Will never look at another woman's butt.

Yes! It's out of line
To think of you 24/7
All of the time.

Yes! It's too much for you
To come to my job every day
And have lunch.

Yes! I'm tired of screaming
And my voice always being hoarse.

So yes, I want a divorce!

UP CLOSE & PERSONAL

I'm awake, but I'm dreaming
Only 2 go 2 sleep and dream that I am awake
Insomnia or insanity? Only GOD can give me his take

Funny how I can feel so youthful, spontaneous like a kid
Only 2 look at my reflection in the mirror
and see the pain and scars of the life I lived

2 feel one way on the inside, and look 180 degrees on the outside
Sometimes I wish that I had just plain died

I've traveled so short on this road called life
I don't know if these feelings are wrong or right

Personally this travel feels long
My face tells the story
My eyes sing the real sad song
TAKE A LOOK

CONFESSIONS

This is something you beg for him to tell ya.
So here goes one of his biggest failures.
He allowed himself to fall in love with a whore.
She didn't even attempt to paint herself as the girl next door.
From the hood of the car to the gas station floor,
He couldn't get enough of her whispers in his ear.
More! More! More!
More signs than he could count screaming
Danger! Danger! Danger!
But we've all been there.
He convinced himself that he could change her. Wrong!
Damn. He wished he could get through some of this anger.
Could have, should have, wishing he should have, never did.
Worst of all is now they share a kid.

JUNKYARD

She found him in a junkyard
The tag around his neck read "just disregard"
That he's useless
He's dumb, a thug, and also clueless

She watched him lying in the snow starting 2 shiver
Ironically at the same time, she felt her heart quiver
She wiped away the frozen tear from his eye
Doing her best not to cry

She cleaned him up and brought him into her life
20 years later she is still his wife
Until this day that's one great romance
Sometimes all a thug needs is a chance.

NOTHING LASTS

Good things seldom last
So enjoy before it becomes the past
Nothing lasts
They just turn into memories
So enjoy before they become history
Nothing lasts
Even though no one asked
That's my conclusion
Good things in life
Are just an illusion
Nothing lasts

RUNAWAY

Do I run away to a place
Where everybody knows my name?
A place where I grew up and played childhood games?

You wonder why I wish to escape
My unknown to your reality.
Is it the principality?
I'll scream it's irrelevant
Let's just say I should have stayed celibate.

Run away.
The thought is tempting and in my mind it hovers
To a place of youthful dreams, family, and past lovers.

Do I return as the moon does night after night?
Do I return such as a bird's journey
south on its fall flight?

Do I return as each Sunday returns after Saturday?
Do I return to a place oh so many miles away?

Today, this place I miss.
Yesterday, this place I wanted to stray.
Do I run away . . .

To Indianapolis?

HIMSELF

He raised himself with no help
Twice in his life you had the
Audacity to use your belt?
Did you think he would respect
Your so-called father figure?
When in reality another black man
Another Nigga!

Call it pain, frustration, or hurt
But there will never be
A World's Greatest Dad present
From him on a T-shirt!

Keeping such a big secret
So young in his life
Knowing you were kissing his Mother
As well as your Wife!

ANGEL

He's an angel living in hell
How does he know?
Because all the people living wrong
Are the same people doing well?
The people that attempt to live right
Are the same ones losing jobs, homes, and can't sleep at night
He hears the dark side calling
And so he's thinking of becoming an angel that has fallen

'80S KINGS

First off, Ice Cube, I want to thank ya
For relating to me when you wrote "Gangsta Gangsta"
Next, Melle Mel and Grand Master Flash for utilizing the talent
that GOD allowed you to use
And you expressed it in every verb that you said and every noun
that you used
Also UTFO for being the first to show me a ho (Roxanne)
Can't forget LL Cool J
For showing me that you can be a businessman
and yet still play and have it your way
Much love always to Ice T
Damn near every song you wrote I felt it was for me
When I first heard and saw Salt-N-Pepa
All that I could say was GOD help ya
For years I thought being a romantic that I was the one and only
Until I heard M. C. Shan's "Left Me Lonely"
I want to thank Too Short for bringing out freaky tales
If not for that I would not have had the nerve
to get the prom queen named Roshell
And for keeping it gangster and yet intelligent
I want to thank B. D. P. for keeping it legit
And so many others from the '80s game
Like Whodini, Sugar Hill, and Dane Dane

TRENDS

Why does everything we do negative tend to set trends?
We have white kids calling each other nigga and fighting over colors.
Why don't we substitute the N word and call each other brother?
We have white kids fighting over colors 2 the end.
Why don't they fight over what black college that they attend.
Now that would be a trend.
I'm glad times have changed and color lines are starting to blend.
At the same time I'm not happy over seeing our negative trends being reflected in the white kids.
Maybe I'm getting old or maybe it's beyond me.
But it shouldn't be a trend to air our dirty laundry.
Now to keep it real, I have a biracial kid.
But I will be damn if I see my past actions reflected in the way he lives.

WISH (OR DO I?)

I had wished I had a car like that!
But a lot of people wish they had a car like mine.
I wish I had a woman like that.
Though many men wished their hearts out
that they had a woman like mine.
I had wished I had a house like that.
Though many had wished they had a house,
much less a house like mine.
Do you feel me?

HANGMAN

I am in the shower,
But there is no soap.
On the pole, a shower curtain used to hang,
Now there is a rope.

Water streams down my body and face.
Only this time the water
Has a salty taste.

I can see the bathtub mat,
Only my feet do not touch it.
They dangle in the air,
Just a few inches above it.

This is my soul,
Looking at my flesh.
It's not water running down my body,
It's tears trickling down my chest.

I was born naked, alone, and crying.
How ironic that this
Is how I would end up dying.

"WOW"

With her eyes she flaunts.
With her eyes she taunts.
I try my damnedest but can't prevail to act nonchalant.
Extraordinary hair that flows luminous,
Eyes that seem to glow . . .
Mix in a smile that daily seems to grow!
With most women their beauty stops right there.
That is what makes competition none
Because no other dares to compare.
Her beauty, that's one thing,
Yet her inner beauty . . .
That's what makes her complete!
In a word — "Elite."
Not to know her is not to understand.
Equivalent to explaining how to catch a rainbow
In the palm of your hand.

Oh, so thankful the Lord allowed Beauty like this to cross my path, and her I did not miss.
It does my heart good to know a woman like this does exist!

To Lingerie Girl.

CAN'T STOP

He watered his plant seed for two months
Yet it didn't grow so he quit

He lifted barbells for a year
Yet he saw little growth so he quit

He worked two jobs for six months
Yet he couldn't reach his goals so he quit

He loved her for three years
Yet she didn't love him back

How come he couldn't quit?

YOU TELL ME!

I know I don't look as good as him.
But I've been there 200% for our child.
Don't that count for anything?

I know I don't have as much money as him.
But I've been there 200% for you.
Don't that count for anything?

I know I don't have as many assets as him.
But I've been there 200% to hold your hand through the worst
times of your Life!
Don't that count for anything?

I know I didn't Graduate High School, but I can Count!
You went to College so tell me, what's the amount?
P.S. Was it worth it when you found out he lied
and his Checks bounced?

LOOKING AHEAD

To the next woman that comes into my life.
I will look at you like a star from near and far.

You will shine so bright in my life.
No hesitating to treat you as my future wife.

Always showing my love on a daily basis,
No matter what the race is.

No drama, just dramatic,
A relationship bursting with intensity, plus trust.
And it's a given,
That I will be romantic.

I swear!

ARE YOU AFRAID?

Why do you jump from
relationship to relationship so fast?
Do you wear a neck brace from having whiplash?
Are you afraid of the dark?
Are you afraid of sleeping alone?
Do you feel more like a woman
to have a man sleeping in your home?
Are you afraid of the dark?
Why is your heart so numb?
And where does this come from?
Are you afraid of the dark?
So tell me your need
To be protected
Her answer: As a child
She was molested

REGRETS

Please don't go!
I promise no mo', no mo', no mo'.
Please stay, I can't imagine you leaving.
Can I borrow one of your tampons,
because I can feel my heart bleeding!
I'm on my knees begging you, please don't go!
I'm about to wrap myself around you
like you're a Christmas present and I'm the bow.
Please don't go!
I promise from now on to treat you like an equal.
I know if you walk out that door there will be no sequel.
Please don't get into that car!
I promise from here on out to raise the bar.
Please don't drive through that gate!
Don't let this be my fate.
Please come back!
I promise to straighten up my act.
Oh, so you're just going to do me like that?
So that's how this ends with you driving away?
That's cool! I didn't like your fat ass anyway!
What's this? It can't be me about to cry!
Oh yeah, it's just the carbon monoxide in my eye! . . .
Isn't it?

ROSALINDA

You always wondered why your Mother treated you
different from your siblings, and what that was all about.
And when you turned 13, it was horrible the news you
found out!
Your Mother was Raped
and that's how you were Conceived
Now you're dealing with your Brother being
Murdered at the age of 18.
Your Sister's living in the same house with her fatherless
kids that total 3,
I can't Fathom how you stayed sane in the mix of all the
Insanity.
But instead of using it as a Crutch
and getting tangled up in a web made of stress.
You cleverly turned it inside out
and made it the secret of your Success
You've somehow taken the cold blizzard of your life
And magically turned it into a Popsicle.
At such a young age you've already endured
some of life's most difficult obstacles.
You will finish life's race a winner because you were
set up as a Loser at the start!
Rosalinda, keep your Head up
until you cross the Finish Line.
And remember God definitely has his Hand on your Heart!

RARE FIND

America the beautiful, America the free
As the sun rose I had no clue of what America had in
Store 4 me
You know what I saw today in a tucked away place?
A woman that had angel written all over her face
In a small snuggled-away town in the heart of Texas
As rare as a hummingbird in the palm of your hand,
I'm sure it would be impossible to catch this
If you wonder to yourself where did I find her
Surprising to me also, working in a truck stop diner
A diamond in the rough, a diamond that's uncut
As rare as a gold mine in Africa that's been untouched
A beauty and elegance that could never be dismissed
I can only imagine if Hollywood gets a hold of this
If that moment were a tape I would constantly rewind it
It just shows that in the middle of nowhere,
GOD'S beauty, you can always find it

ALONE

Am I meant 2 B alone or is this just a phase
Searching 4 A companion
sometimes can feel like I'm lost in a maze
I need that woman 2 B my lighthouse and guide me home
Please don't leave me in this maze lost, scared, and alone
I am searching 4 love I am searching 4 u
Love at first sight, is it true or am I just a fool?

COWARD?

From the cradle to the grave,
And from the grave back to the womb,
Reincarnation, some say it's not true.

In my past life I must have been a King,
Because this lifetime
Poverty and suffering is all
That my eyes see.

Too much of a coward
To wish for death.
Though this lifetime is a travesty,
The next lifetime could really bring regrets.

Coward?

SILENT NIGHT

Silent night
Holy night
She slit her wrists on Christmas Eve
because she has no life
Merry Christmas to all and to all a good night

"NO TRUST, NO PEACE"

"Trust is the Foundation"
But my heart, soul, and spirit
Scream, "Perpetration!"

What should be there
Is simply not.
What should not be there
Is undeniably present.

How long can I go on
your words that it's just irrelevant?

"No Trust, No Peace"
Things that were hid in the past
Are the same things that are slowly
Uncovering now!

I wonder every day what's really
Going on behind that smile.
For years we were friends,
But know too much about one another's past.
That's why this potential love
Won't stand a chance!!

No Trust,
No Peace.

DEAR GOD

Here is a letter that I once wrote.
A list of things in my unbalanced life
That are broke.

My heart, soul, pockets, and spirit.
Maybe it's lost in the mail,
Or maybe you did not read it.

Maybe it's sitting on a desk
In a stack of many.
From my understanding,
That if I asked I would receive plenty.

Maybe I put the wrong zip code,
And it went to another zone.
Because it seems it didn't reach your throne.
But somehow wound up
In the devil's home.

END TIMES

Why do people keep coming to me crying,
Saying that it's the end of times?
They have been saying that it's the end of times since the beginning of the world!
It's not as if grown men were starting to rape preteen girls.
And they say it's the end of times.
It's not as if Catholic priests started molesting altar boys.
Or every corner store started selling sex toys.
And they say it's the end of times.
It's not as if suburban teenagers were murdering their daddies and mothers.
It's not as if inner-city youth were killing each other over colors.
And they say it's the end of times.
That sounds as crazy to me as people were dying by simply having intercourse.
Or as crazy as being able to turn on the Internet and see a woman having sex with a horse.
And they say it's the end of times.

WITHDRAW

3:45 a.m. my body shakes
But it's not from the alcohol
It's you my body calls
My heart quivers
My soul shivers
Your love is the drug
I need the dope man to deliver
It's not nicotine but the scent
Of your perfume I want to inhale
A second chance is all I ask
And I promise not to fail
I wish there was a 12-step program
To show you I am meant
To be your man
Only for me you are the equivalent
Of ecstasy
This is a travesty
So sad
I wonder is there a Betty Ford clinic
For this type of rehab?

FRIEND OR FOE—(HO)

I'm sitting in your living room watching the game with my
boy and I glance over at you in the kitchen
dicing onions.
I can't believe you came on to me the other night and you
know my boy is your husband.

20/20 hindsight, I should have never continued to get
closer 2 U once you told me your relationship was sinking.
20/20 hindsight, I should have never accepted your
Invitation to a bar when it was obvious
you had already been drinking.

Though in the beginning I can honestly say
I didn't see the Signs,
But once I stopped, hit pause, and then hit Rewind,

It was clear as a Window without a Pane.
But I couldn't understand what did you have to gain?
I was too blinded by my own conceitedness, not seeing
that your attempting to get with me
was your own way of
getting back at He.

But what did he do to make you stoop to this level?
So I started digging so deep I needed a Hard Hat and a
Shovel!
But O-My-God what did I uncover?
Come to find out he was trying to get with my Lover!

So, here I sit on the couch in between he and she.
What do I do, do I fight?
Or do I wait till he goes to work and come back tonight?

How do I defend
When I'm caught between two sins?

WASTED YOUTH

Replaying my childhood terrifies me
As a grown man.
So how did I manage as a teen?
I just don't understand.
I guess youth is wasted on the young,
How dumb.

If I could just take some of that
Invisibility plus inferiorism
And transplant it into this grown man spirit.

Maaaaaan, the possibilities, but my maturity
Just doesn't want to hear it.
Now there's too much to lose,
Not wanting that alarm clock to buzz,
But too scared to hit snooze.

When did I become so fragile?
Where did I get so cautious?
Once one of the hardest boys in town
Just as my virginity
Somehow I lost it.

Though extremely thankful for the maturity
The Lord has instilled upon me.
Though every now and again
I wish for what I lost,
Including my virginity.

IN STYLE

In the early '80s you passed me by
simply because I didn't look like El DeBarge
I was too hard

In the mid '80s you passed me by
simply because I didn't have green eyes
It's true, don't lie

Fast-forward to the early '90s
you passed me by simply because I wasn't dark-skinned
like Wesley Snipes or Michael Jordan
Yes, it's still me that you're ignoring

Only a few years later you passed me by
simply because I did not sell dope
Damn, is there any hope?

Now the late '90s and beyond,
you can't be mad because I pass you by
because you're not from the Islands, Asian, or White

Karma Is a Bitch!!!

ONE LAST BREATH

Here I am down to one last breath again
Me, my soul, and spirit
I wonder how many times I can get down
Then at the last second get up
Take the last breath before I go down for good
It's been done so much that it's natural
But at some point I won't take that 2nd breath
I won't get a 2nd chance
Once again I wonder "Is this It?"

P.S.—Is this my life
Or the start of my death?

To be continued . . .

SIGHT UNSEEN

Have you ever felt the breeze
Fresh, skimming across the tops of the ocean?

Have you ever watched a wave elevate in
Height, only to demise its motion?

Have you ever counted each of the sun's rays
Reflected on the sea's surface?

Neither have I.

How many black men have?

Maybe that's a fraction of the problem . . .

WE SHINE IN THE DARK

Newly discovered beautiful plants on the lowest surface of the ocean
In total darkness never seeing any sunlight
And yet they shine so bright
All these years and never been discovered
Like they were playing hide-and-seek and the ocean was their cover
No sun rays and yet so full of color
It makes you wonder
No matter where you are, no matter if no one sees you
You are always beautiful
Even in total darkness
GOD always makes you shine.

SEASONS

Everything that happens in your life
There is a reason
Your life is just like the weather
There are 4 seasons.
Spring, summer, winter, and fall
You have to stay strong and endure them all
Like the rosebush that suffers through the winter wind
Once the seasons change now it's spring
And it does bloom again.
I know the winters are harsh and cold
The summers are brutal and hot
Just keep your roots strong and grounded
And <u>God</u> will fail you not
These are the Seasons of your life
Let God's promise keep you warm on this winter's night.

REFLECTIONS

Today I passed a group of boys walking along the side of the freeway
Not attending school because today is a Holiday
In their hands they carried fishing poles
Apparently just leaving a fishing hole
I glance in the rearview mirror to look behind
In one of their smiling faces I see mine
Long before I ever picked up a gun to shoot
I was just an innocent youth
Oh how I wish that I could put that car in reverse
And walk with the youngsters laughing and joking over and over as
If it were rehearsed
With candy on our breath, rocks in our pockets, and no worries of
Tomorrow on our mind
As my life played out that day . . . oh do I wish that I could hit
Rewind

CANDY

I've liked candy since I was a kid, but now I'm grown I like a different kind.
I like the candy you can lick from front and behind.
You real lovers out there know what I mean.
Some candy comes wrapped in tight apple bottom jeans.
Some candy comes wrapped in tight miniskirts.
But I won't touch candy if candy touched dirt.
C.A.N.D.Y. See I love candy and I won't lie.
It's got a hole in the middle like a lifesaver.
And the candy I love comes in all kinds of flavors.
I don't believe a good thing should go to waste.
And the candy I love is an acquired taste.
I like it hot, slippery, and wet.
And girls just can't wait until I put it to the test.
(C.A.N.D.Y.)

I'm like a bloodhound, baby, when I smell the scent.
And until I find it, I won't quit.
I cross mountains, and I cross over seas.
I'll do anything, girl, just to get a piece.
And once I catch 'em, I know that I've got 'um.
How many licks does it take to get to the bottom?
But there's no need to rush much.
You will get wet and you will slip and slide.
So just hold on tight and enjoy the ride.
If your candy is good, then you can be my queen.
Some people might call me a Candy Fiend.
On the corner of my neighborhood, I'll set up a booth
For people like me with a sweet tooth (C.A.N.D.Y.)

The women love it, because they can't seem to get enough.
But I guess I was blessed with a gentle touch.
And when it comes to candy, if I had my choice.
I'd choose sweet, I'd choose chocolate, and I'd choose moist.
We can do it anywhere girl. In any room.
But just do me one favor and don't come too soon.
Hell yeah, I'm freaky, without a doubt.
But I still love it melted in my hand and not in my mouth.
So after I'm done, please give me time . . .
To close my eyes and come down . . .
From my sugar high.
(C.A.N.D.Y.)

YOUNG BOYS

Young boys, make sure you listen
Young boys, make sure you do not miss this
When you talk about a woman's vagina, you talk about beating it up
Young boys listen up
That lovely thing was not put here for you to beat up
It's not a black man, and you're not the police
Young boys, you need to learn how to caress, massage her chest
Give more and not less
Young boys, you brag about at least you get yours
But you wonder what that vibrating noise behind the bathroom door is

YOUNG BOYS, STOP IMITATING A THUG

Learn how to make love
Stop trying to beat it up until it's numb
If it's done right, she's left in a fetal position sucking her thumb
Young boys, don't beat it up
Maybe you should try eating it up
Young boys

HALF-MAST

I pledge allegiance to the flag of the Bang! Bang! Bang!
Allow me to address the President, Congress, also you and your work staff
From here on out, keep your American flags at half-mast
There is no need to raise them back to the top
Because in a couple of days they will have to drop
Due to someone mentally ill or due to an ignorant crook
It's inevitable there will be another Sandy Hook
Keep Flags at half-mast
Though it's hellacious, it's inevitable there will be another
South Carolina church shooting by a racist
Not sending my child to college was something I'd thought I would always regret
But now sadly to say, ask that of the parents of the kids from Virginia Tech
Flags at half-mast

BLESSED

I am so blessed to live in an America without boundaries
To see so many different races finding love with one another all around me
What did all the hatred accomplish in the past?
I'm just blessed to live in a time where that did not last
America losing its racism that's almost funny
Next we need to work on living in an America where it's not about money
One step at a time
For mankind